SCIENCE SUPPORT
Physics

HELEN NORRIS

CAMBRIDGE
UNIVERSITY PRESS

PUBLISHED BY THE PRESS SYNDICATE OF THE UNIVERSITY OF CAMBRIDGE
The Pitt Building, Trumpington Street, Cambridge, United Kingdom

CAMBRIDGE UNIVERSITY PRESS
The Edinburgh Building, Cambridge CB2 2RU, UK
40 West 20th Street, New York, NY 10011–4211, USA
477 Williamstown Road, Port Melbourne, VIC 3207, Australia
Ruiz de Alarcón 13, 28014 Madrid, Spain
Dock House, The Waterfront, Cape Town 8001, South Africa

http://www.cambridge.org

First published 1997
Reprinted 1998, 2002, 2003

Printed in the United Kingdom at the University Press, Cambridge

Design and illustration by Hardlines, Charlbury

Typeface Avant Garde and Adobe Caslon 12/15 pt

A catalogue record for this book is available from the British Library

ISBN 0 521 57913 9

Notice to teachers

Acknowledgement
The Hertfordshire Science Teaching Scholarships provided the opportunity
for the author to begin with the *Science Support* work.

Contents

FORCES AND MOTION

WAVES AND RADIATION

Teacher's Notes

AIM

The overall aim of the *Science Support* materials is to allow pupils with learning difficulties to achieve success in science at Key Stage 4. This is done in several ways:

- Presenting the material at an appropriate level means that barriers are removed which might prevent pupils from interacting with the subject.

- New concepts are introduced in small steps, with frequent repetition and reinforcement in a variety of ways.

- Revision exercises help to familiarise pupils with essential foundation work.

- Opportunities are provided for pupils to further develop their literacy skills in the classroom, using subject-related matter.

- The materials are designed to suit a *band* of low-ability pupils, so that the least able pupils can be given the same activity as those of higher ability. This means that the least able pupils do not feel singled out in any way.

- Less able pupils are provided with sufficient information about each topic to allow them to contribute to group work.

- Pupils are encouraged to interact with the information that they are given, i.e. they are required to make a response to the text by underlining something, putting information into a table, etc.

INTRODUCTION

- The *Science Support* materials are a teacher's resource, and are designed to be used in a number of ways. The ways in which the worksheets are used are as important as the worksheets themselves.

- Instructions have been omitted from many of the worksheets to give the teacher the flexibility to use the activity in a variety of ways. This also allows the teacher to decide if he/she wants the pupils to write on the sheet. The teacher could add further instruction to the sheets prior to photocopying if desired. Some of the ways in which the sheets can be used are described in the section 'How to use the worksheets'.

- Many of the worksheets are for reinforcement and repetition. It is essential that these are not given to the pupils 'cold', i.e. some preparatory work should already have been done on the topic. Exceptions to this are the 'linkword' sheets which can be used as diagnostic tools, i.e. the teacher can use them to assess a pupil's prior knowledge of a subject (see page 17).

- Though designed to be used at Key Stage 4, teachers may be tempted to use some of the worksheets at Key Stage 3. It is suggested that teachers avoid this so that when used at Key Stage 4, the activities are fresh and therefore stimulating to the pupils.

- Many of the worksheets have been designed to be used in pairs. In a number of cases one of the sheets in a pair will be disposable (i.e. the pupil will write on it) while the other sheet could be reused. To improve the presentation and life expectancy of the reusable sheets, they could be laminated.

HOW TO USE THE WORKSHEETS

Word lists

Most pupils with learning difficulties have a basic literacy problem, for example spelling and/or reading.

- The word lists can be used as a spelling reference for pupils.

- Teachers can add their own words to the lists, if they wish to do so.

- If the support teacher or special-needs teacher is aware of the vocabulary the pupil is currently encountering in science, then he/she may be able to use this with the pupil.

- The words can be used as a revision checklist. Prior to a test the teacher can ask pupils to ensure that they know the meanings of all or selected words from the list.

- Pupils can use the words to produce their own puzzles, for example wordsearches and crosswords. Good puzzles can be reproduced for others to use. The more often pupils use the words, the more familiar they will become.

- Pupils should be encouraged to say the words out loud. This will increase their confidence and help them with the spellings of the words.

'Fill in the gaps' exercises

On these worksheets, the words that are required to complete the exercise are usually provided. The sheets could be used by more able pupils if the words are blanked out before photocopying. In this way the 'same' sheet could be used by more of the class.

Some pupils might reasonably be expected to copy out the whole paragraph while it will be more appropriate for others just to 'fill in the gaps'.

Matching exercises/diagram labelling

The activities can be used in a number of ways depending on the ability of the pupils. The least able pupils may prefer to do them as 'cut and stick' activities. Others may prefer to write in the information, though this will depend on the size and legibility of their handwriting. A more able pupil could present the information in a different form or expand on it, if he/she is given a relevant textbook.

Directed activities related to text

These worksheets usually consist of a piece of text, a table and/or diagrams which the pupils are expected to read or study carefully. They are accompanied by a series of instructions which the pupils then follow. In this way, the pupils can engage with the information that has been presented to them.

Some worksheets are based upon **ordering and sequencing activities**. These also require the pupils to engage with the information given (written or otherwise) before carrying out the exercise.

Puzzles

Wordsearches and crosswords etc. are designed to be used after the pupils have studied the topic. They are reinforcement or revision activities. Pupils can be encouraged to make up their own puzzles and games, particularly if they are armed with a relevant word list.

Linkword

- Unlike most of the worksheets, these activities have instructions for the pupils to follow.

- Experience shows that pupils need practice using the 'linkword' technique. The first time it is used it is best to use relatively simple concepts which pupils feel confident with.

- Linkword can be used as an assessment tool before or after a topic has been introduced. By using it before a topic begins, the teacher is able to take into account the pupil's prior knowledge when planning the route through the module. This idea is linked to concept mapping.

- Linkword may or may not be accompanied by an information sheet. Pupils can carry out the linkword after reading the sheet to see how much they have understood.

- The linkword can also be used as a way of taking notes on the information given.

- While it is never desirable to overuse a technique that apparently works well, it is relatively simple for other linkwords to be designed wherever appropriate.

Practical sheets

Pupils with learning difficulties often need help to:

- record results;

- structure the writing-up of experiments.

The instructions and diagrams on the worksheets deliberately contain a minimum amount of information and do not encompass all of the safety aspects that the teacher would be expected to cover with the pupils. It would be foolish to rely on written warnings for pupils with learning difficulties – this type of information is best given verbally. It is essential, therefore, that the sheets are used purely to supplement the verbal information given to the pupils during their practical work.

Where sheets do not include some part of the experimental process, for example the conclusion, the teacher may wish to cover this with the pupils in some other way.

In the investigation *Keeping the water warm* (pages 51 and 52), the names of the insulating materials to be used are left to the teacher's discretion. One way to differentiate this activity would be to give less able pupils, say, two materials to compare while pupils of higher ability could tackle four or five.

REQUIREMENTS FOR PRACTICAL ACTIVITIES

Electricity and magnetism

3 Conductors and insulators
Each group will require:

- apparatus to make a lamp light in a simple circuit (Worcester circuit board or similar)
- a variety of conducting materials, e.g. copper, aluminium, iron, brass
- a variety of insulating materials, e.g. wood, plastic, glass

7 Lamps in series
Each group will require:

- apparatus to make two lamps light in a simple series circuit (Worcester circuit board or similar)
- ammeter, preferably digital

8 Lamps in parallel
Each group will require:

- apparatus to make two lamps light in a simple parallel circuit (Worcester circuit board or similar)
- ammeter, preferably digital

18 Magnets
Each group will require:

- 2 bar magnets, with the North and South poles marked in some way
- 2 clamp stands
- thread or thin string

22A Using magnets to make a motor
Each group will require:

- kit for making a motor
- power supply (4 V d.c.)

It is advisable to practise making the motor before the lesson as there are many pitfalls.

24 Using magnets to make electricity
Each group will require:

- kit for making a dynamo (same as that for making a motor)
- voltmeter and leads to attach it to the dynamo

Energy and the Earth

4 Convection

This is best performed as a demonstration.

- large (1 litre) Pyrex beaker
- Bunsen burner
- tripod
- gauze
- heatproof mat

To show the movement of the water prior to heating, a crystal of potassium manganate(VII) can be carefully introduced into the beaker as shown below.

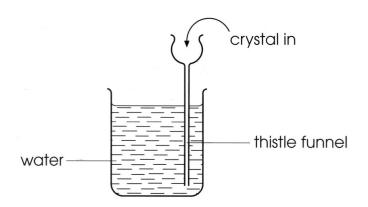

11A Keeping the water warm

Each group will require:

- at least one copper beaker
- a selection of insulating materials, e.g. cotton wool, foam rubber, woollen fabric, newspaper, polyester wadding
- methods for fixing the insulation, e.g. rubber bands, adhesive tape
- access to hot water, e.g. kettle or tap
- thermometer
- stopclock or stopwatch

11B Keeping the water warm

Each group will require:

- at least one copper beaker (preferably two)
- thick layer of insulating material, e.g. foam rubber
- 2 thin layers of same insulating material
- methods for fixing the insulation, e.g. rubber bands, adhesive tape
- access to hot water, e.g. kettle or tap
- thermometer
- stopclock or stopwatch

Forces and motion

8A Using a ticker timer
Each group will require:

- a ticker timer
- power supply (6 V a.c.)
- self-adhesive ticker tape *or* ticker tape and glue

9A Getting faster
Each group will require:

- a ticker timer
- power supply (6 V a.c.)
- self-adhesive ticker tape *or* ticker tape and glue
- a trolley
- elastic with rings on to pull trolley

9B Getting faster
Each group will require:

- a ticker timer
- power supply (6 V a.c.)
- self-adhesive ticker tape *or* ticker tape and glue
- a trolley
- 3 elastics with rings on to pull trolley

9C Getting faster
Each group will require:

- a ticker timer
- power supply (6 V a.c.)
- self-adhesive ticker tape *or* ticker tape and glue
- 2 trolleys
- elastic with rings on to pull trolleys

ANSWERS TO WORDSEARCHES

Energy and the Earth

10 Energy transfer

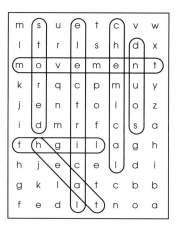

15 Renewable energy

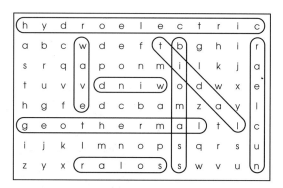

17 Planets wordsearch

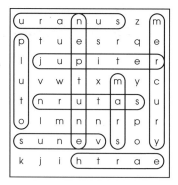

Waves and radiation

5 Lightword

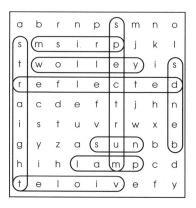

Electricity and magnetism

1 Electricity and magnetism word list

A acetate
ammeter
amps
appliance
attract

B battery

C cell
charge
circuit
coil
conductor
current

D dynamo

E earth
economy
electricity
electromagnet
energy

F fuse

G

H

I insulation
insulator
iron

J

K

L lamp
light
live

M magnet
measure
motor

N neutral
North

O

P parallel
plug
pole
power

Q

R repel
resistance
resistor

S safety
series
South
static
switch
symbol

T transformer

U

V voltage
voltmeter

W wire

X, Y, Z

2 Symbols

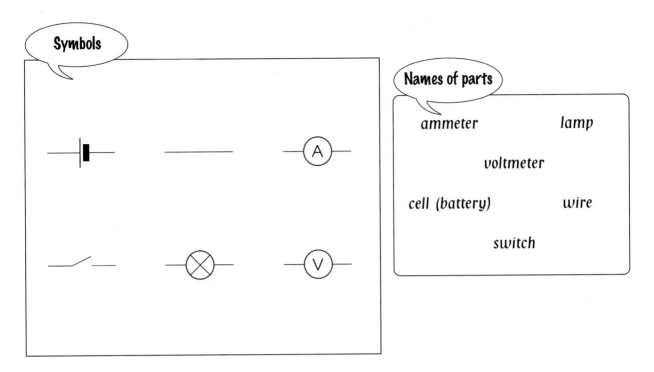

Symbols

Names of parts

ammeter   lamp

voltmeter

cell (battery)   wire

switch

Name of part	Symbol	What it does
		This stores energy which can be changed into electricity.
		This carries the current from one part of the circuit to another.
		This measures the voltage.
		This makes a gap in the circuit. It can be open or closed.
		This measures the current.
		This transfers electrical energy to light energy.

3 Conductors and insulators

- Cut out the boxes and put them in the right order.

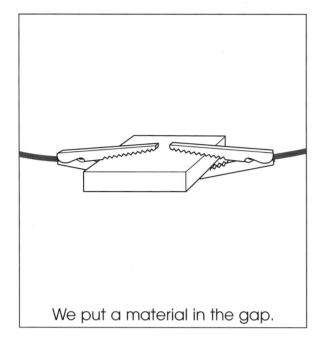

We put a material in the gap.

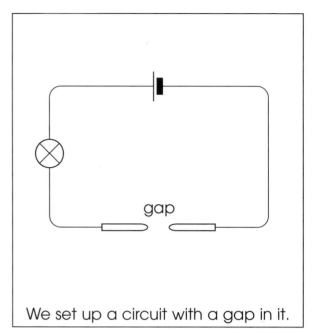

We set up a circuit with a gap in it.

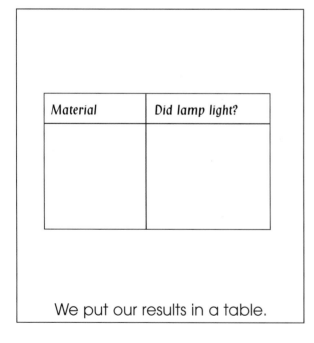

Material	Did lamp light?

We put our results in a table.

We looked to see if the lamp lit up.

What we found out

Some materials will allow the lamp to light, for example _____ .

We call these materials **conductors**.

Some materials will not allow the lamp to light, for example _____ .

We call these materials **insulators**.

4 Series and parallel

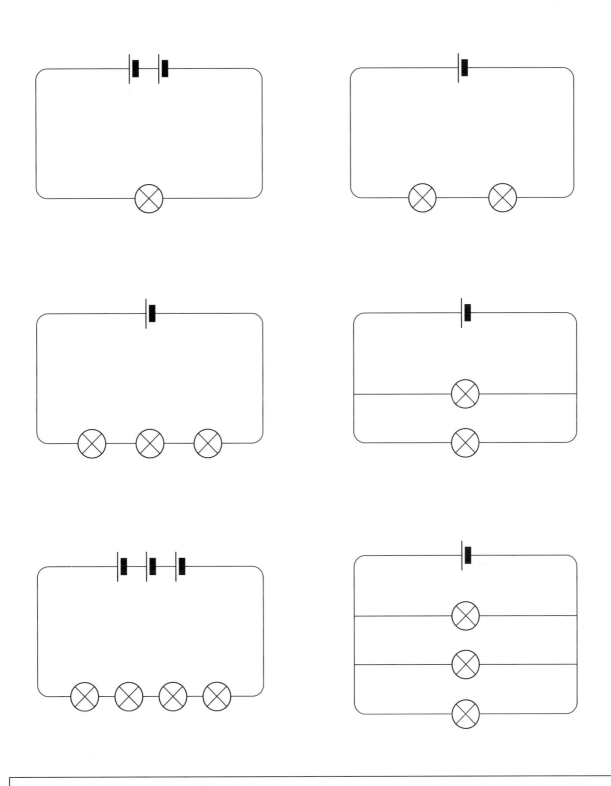

A   two cells in series

B   two lamps in series

C   two lamps in parallel

D   three lamps in series

E   three lamps in parallel

F   three cells in series

5 Measuring current

We use an **ammeter** to measure **current**.

We measure electric current in units called **amperes** (or amps).

We must connect the ammeter **in series** with the circuit.

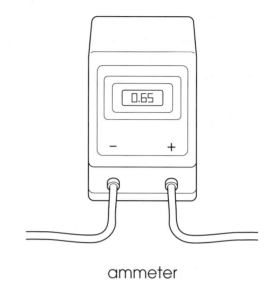

ammeter

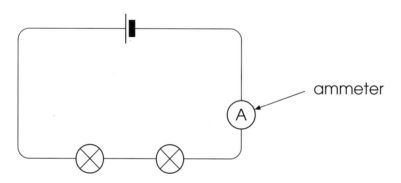

ammeter

Using an ammeter

An ammeter measures ...	
The symbol for an ammeter is ...	
We always connect it in ...	
Electric current is measured in units called ...	

6 Measuring voltage

A **voltmeter** measures the 'push' of a battery. Some batteries can push harder than others. A battery with a large push has a big **voltage**.

We measure voltage in units called **volts**.

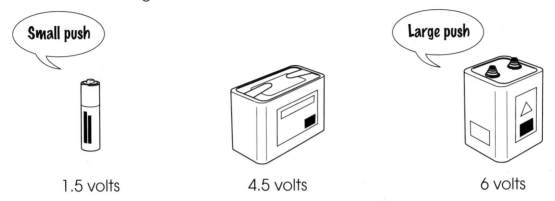

Small push   Large push

1.5 volts   4.5 volts   6 volts

To measure the voltage of a battery we must connect the voltmeter **in parallel** with it.

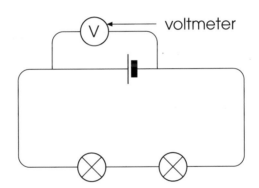

voltmeter

Using a voltmeter

A voltmeter measures ...	
The symbol for a voltmeter is ...	
We always connect it in ...	
We measure voltage in units called ...	

7 Lamps in series

- Set up these circuits.

X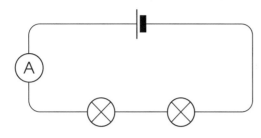

ammeter reading _____ A
(current)

Y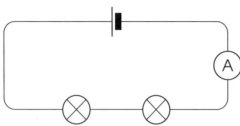

ammeter reading _____ A
(current)

Z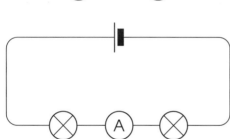

ammeter reading _____ A
(current)

- Now put your results in the table below.

Ammeter position	Current (amps)
X	
Y	
Z	

What we found out

When lamps are joined **in series**, the current flowing is the (**same/different**) in each part of the circuit.

8 Lamps in parallel

- Set up these circuits.

P

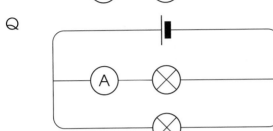

ammeter reading _____ A
(current)

Q

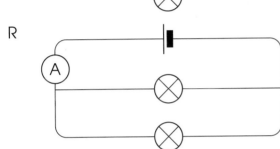

ammeter reading _____ A
(current)

R

ammeter reading _____ A
(current)

- Now put your results in the table below.

Ammeter position	Current (amps)
P	
Q	
R	

What we found out

When lamps are joined **in parallel**, the current to the ammeter in positions
P and Q is the (**same/different**).

If we add together the currents in the branches we find that they _____

_____ .

9 Electricity – linkword

❶ Cut out each of the word patches below.

❷ Arrange them on a large piece of paper.

❸ Draw lines between the words if you can think of something that links them.

❹ Write on the lines if it makes the link clearer.

Example:

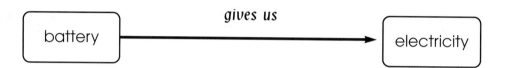

❺ When you have made as many links as you can, stick the word patches down on the paper.

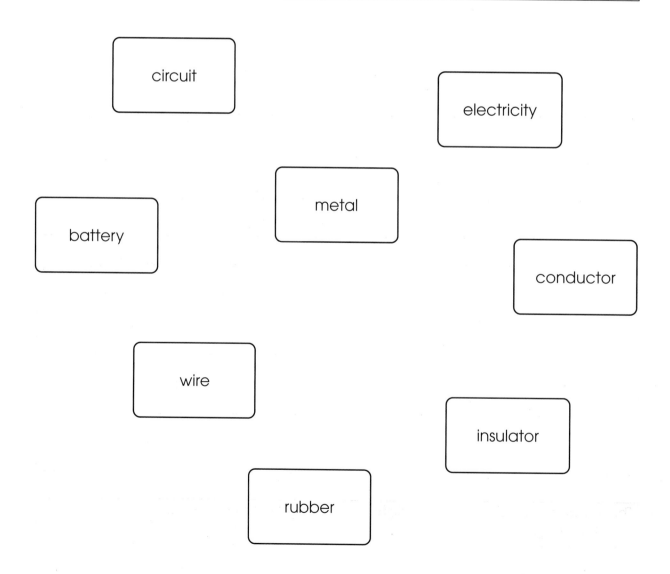

10 What changes?

- Look at the diagrams below. Circuits A, B and C are different because

_____

_____ .

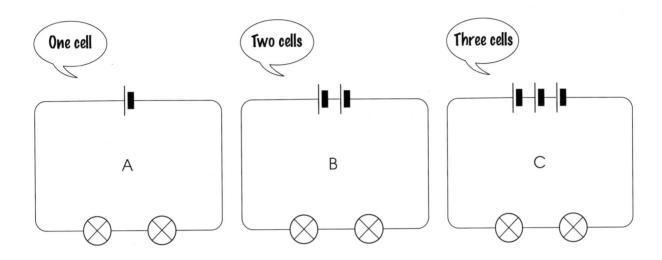

- Look at the table below. Circuits A, B and C are also different because

_____

_____ .

Circuit	How bright are the lamps?
A	dim
B	bright
C	very bright

The **number of cells** and the **brightness of the lamps** are the **factors** which change.

11A Using electricity

	Colour	What the appliance does
Key		It transfers energy from *electricity* into _____ energy.
		It transfers energy from _____ into _____ energy.
		It transfers energy from _____ into _____ energy.

When an electric current flows through some wires, the wires get hotter. We call these wires **resistance wires**.

Electrical appliances which get hot contain resistance wires, for example electric heaters, toasters and irons.

11B Using electricity

Look at the other sheet.

1 We use electricity to give us **light**. Put a red circle around the things which transfer energy from electricity to light.

2 We use electricity to give us **sound**. Put a blue circle around the things which transfer energy from electricity to sound.

Some things will have two circles around them.

3 We use electricity to give us **heat**. Put a black circle around the things which transfer energy from electricity to heat.

4 Complete the key.

5 Underline in black the sentence which tells you what happens when electric current passes through some wires.

6 Put a box around the name that we give to these wires.

7 Underline in red the names of some appliances which contain resistance wires.

12A Static electricity

Making static electricity

We can make static electricity by rubbing some things together. If we rub a plastic comb with a duster, the comb will pick up tiny pieces of paper.

Different charges

When we rub some things we give them a **charge**. If we rub two pieces of plastic bin bag with a duster they both get the **same** charge.

They push away from each other.

We say that they **repel** each other.

Charge on bin bag is −

When we rub two pieces of acetate with a duster they also repel each other. This is because each piece of acetate gets the same charge.

Charge on acetate is +

But charged acetate and charged bin bag have **different** charges. If we bring them together they **attract** each other.

12B Static electricity

- Look at the other sheet and then complete this table.

Word bank (cloud): attract, repel, same, different

Material	Charge (+ or −)	What happens when we rub two pieces (Draw a diagram to show this.)	Why this happens
bin bag			The two charged pieces of bin bag _____ each other because they have the _____ charge.
acetate			The two charged pieces of acetate _____ each other because they have the _____ charge.

When we bring charged bin bag close to charged acetate they _____ each other.

This is because they have _____ charges.

diagram

13A Fuses

Fuses can prevent fires. They can also stop your electrical appliances from being damaged. An electrical appliance is something which uses electricity, like a kettle or a hair dryer.

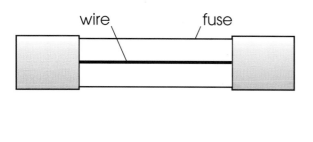

There is a thin piece of wire inside a fuse. It can only carry a certain amount of current.

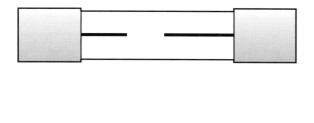

If too much electricity passes through the wire it will melt or 'blow'. Current can't pass through the 'blown' fuse. The appliance stops working.

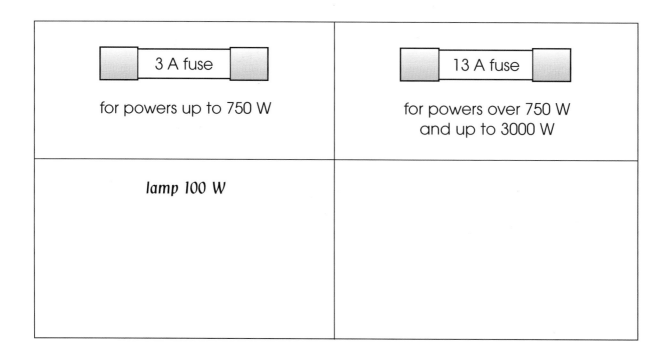

3 A fuse	13 A fuse
for powers up to 750 W	for powers over 750 W and up to 3000 W
lamp 100 W	

13B Fuses

Use the other sheet to answer these questions.

1 Underline in red the **two** reasons why we use fuses.

2 Underline in black what we find inside a fuse.

3 Underline in blue the sentence which tells you what makes a fuse 'blow'.

4 Label the diagrams of the fuses using these words:

a fuse which will work   *a blown fuse*

5 Fill in the table to say which fuse you need for these appliances.
The first one is done for you.

lamp 100 W

fridge 150 W

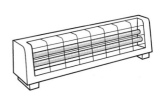

electric fire 1000 W

drill 360 W

toaster 900 W

CD player 200 W

iron 800 W

kettle 2000 W

14 Which wire?

live	neutral
earth	

This is the dangerous wire. _____

This wire will stop you from getting an electric shock
if your appliance is damaged. _____

This wire is covered in brown insulation. _____

In a plug, this wire is connected to the fuse. _____

This wire is covered in green and yellow insulation. _____

This wire is there for safety reasons. _____

This wire is covered in blue insulation. _____

We need this wire if an appliance has a metal case. _____

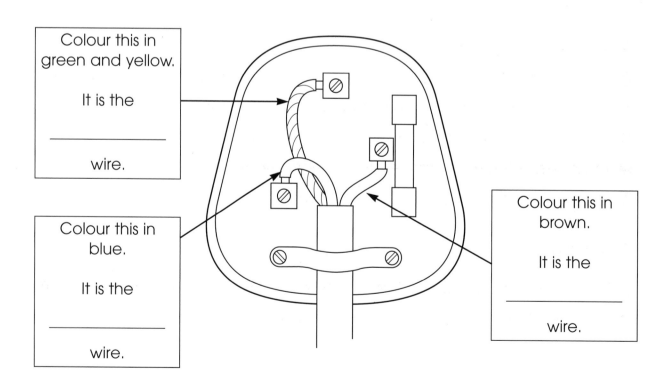

Colour this in
green and yellow.

It is the

_____

wire.

Colour this in
blue.

It is the

_____

wire.

Colour this in
brown.

It is the

_____

wire.

- Now label the **fuse** on the diagram of the plug.

15 Mainsword

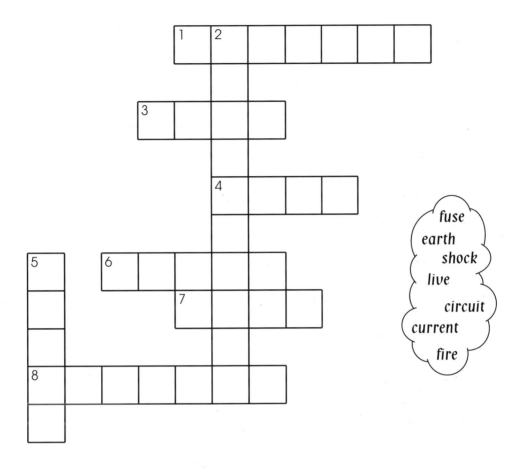

Clues across

1 We can use _____ breakers in place of fuses. (7)

3 This is a thin piece of wire which melts if too much current passes through it. (4)

4 This wire is dangerous. We always connect it to the fuse in a plug. (4)

6 This wire is for safety. It protects you from getting a shock. (5)

7 This is one of the main dangers from electricity. (4)

8 Too much electric _____ 'blows' a fuse. (7)

Clues down

2 This is usually made from rubber or plastic. It is used to cover bare wires. (10)

5 This is another big danger from electricity. (5)

16 Economy 7 electricity

Remember! Economy 7 electricity is only switched on at night.

• Are these sentences **true** or **false**?

Write 'true' or 'false'.

£ £	Economy 7 gives us cheaper electricity than normal.	
	We can use Economy 7 during the day.	
	We can only use Economy 7 for seven hours each night.	
	We can set our washing machine to use Economy 7 electricity.	
	Power stations waste less electricity if we use Economy 7.	
	It is a good idea to use Economy 7 for things which use a lot of electricity, like heating up the water.	
	We can use Economy 7 to heat water up, but we must keep it warm by insulating the hot water tank.	
	Children are using Economy 7 electricity when they watch afternoon television.	

17 Using electricity

We can read the meter to find out how much electricity we use.
The graph shows some meter readings taken over a year.

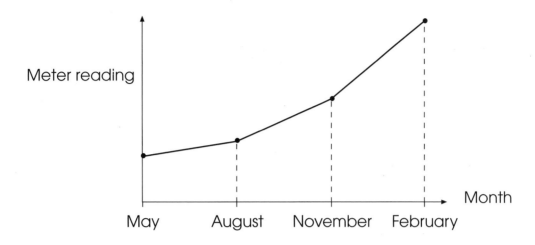

A flat line on the graph tells us that no electricity was used up.

A very steep line on the graph tells us that _____

_____ .

A shallow slope on the graph tells us that _____

_____ .

cold   dark   light   heat

- Look at the graph.

1 A lot of electricity is used between the months of November and February.

This is because _____

_____ .

2 Very little electricity is used between _____ and _____ .

This is because _____

_____ .

18 Magnets

steel		North pole	repel (push away)
	attract (pull together)	iron	South pole

We can make magnets from the metals _____ and _____ .

The ends of a magnet are called the _____ _____

and the _____ _____ .

If we bring two magnets together like

this they will _____

(or _____).

In the box draw what happens to the magnets.

North pole

S   N   N   S

South pole

If we bring two magnets together like

this they will _____

(or _____).

In the box draw what happens to the magnets.

S   N   S   N

19A Electromagnets

How do we make electromagnets?

We can make magnets using electricity. We call them **electromagnets**.

To make a simple electromagnet you can wind copper wire around a large iron nail. When electricity flows through the wire the nail becomes an electromagnet.

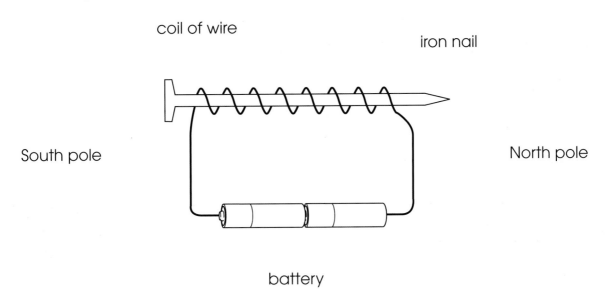

coil of wire

iron nail

South pole

North pole

battery

Electromagnets are useful to us

Ordinary bar magnets keep on working all of the time. Electromagnets are useful because we can switch them on and off. We can make them in all different shapes and sizes.

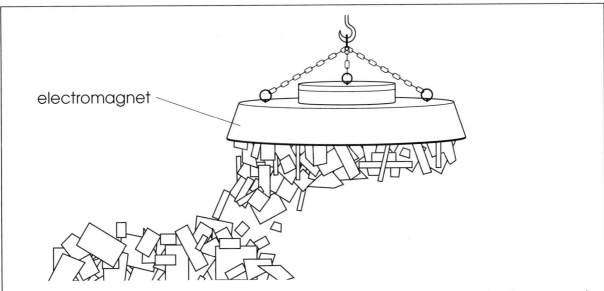

electromagnet

A very large electromagnet is used at a scrapyard. When the electromagnet is switched on it picks up heavy iron. When the electromagnet is switched off, the iron can be dropped where we want it.

19B Electromagnets

Look at the other sheet and then answer these questions.

1 Find the name of a magnet that we make using electricity. Underline it in red.

2 a Join the labels to the diagram.

    b On the diagram, shade in blue the object which becomes a magnet.

    c Draw over the coil of wire in green.

3 Find the sentence which tells us why electromagnets are so useful. Underline it in black.

4 a Underline in red the name of a place where we use electromagnets.

    b In the picture, shade the electromagnet in blue.

5 Copy and complete the table below.

Electromagnet on or off?	What happens to the scrap iron?
on	
	It is dropped where we want it.

20A Making an electromagnet

Jo made an electromagnet using an iron nail.

❶ She passed an electric current through the coil of wire. She tested the electromagnet to see how many paper clips she could pick up.

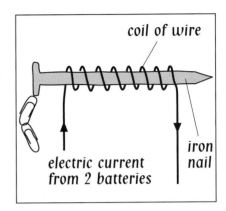

❷ She plotted her results on the graph below.

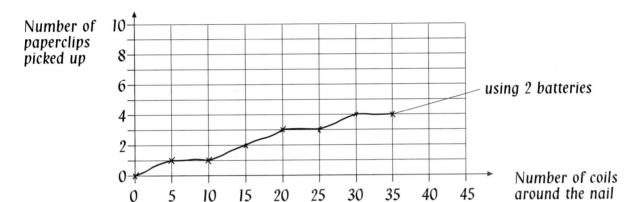

She repeated the experiment using **4** batteries instead of 2.
She put the results in the table below.

Number of coils around the nail	Number of paperclips picked up
0	0
5	2
10	4
15	4
20	5
25	6
30	7
40	8
45	8

20B Making an electromagnet

❶ On the other sheet, plot the results from the table onto Jo's graph.

❷ Join the points up with a red line. Label the new line 'using 4 batteries'.

❸ Using the results from Jo's experiments, complete the sentences below.

We can make an _____ using a nail made

from _____ and a coil of wire.

If we want to make a strong electromagnet we need

a   a (**large/small**) number of coils around the nail

b   (**more/less**) batteries.

❹ Draw a diagram to show how you would make an electromagnet that would pick up more than eight paperclips.

21 Magnets – linkword

1 Cut out each of the word patches below.

2 Arrange them on a large piece of paper.

3 Draw lines between the words if you can think of something that links them.

4 Write on the lines if it makes the link clearer.

Example:

$$\boxed{\text{magnet}} \xrightarrow{\textit{is made from}} \boxed{\text{iron}}$$

5 When you have made as many links as you can, stick the word patches down on the paper.

---

steel

magnet

metal

North pole

iron

attract
(pull together)

South pole

repel
(push away)

22A Using magnets to make a motor

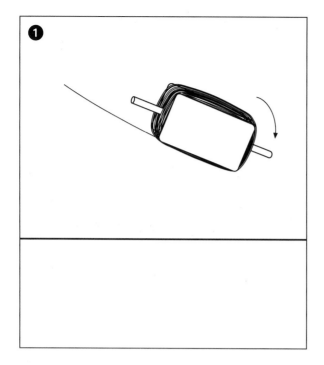

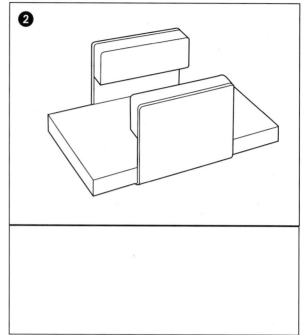

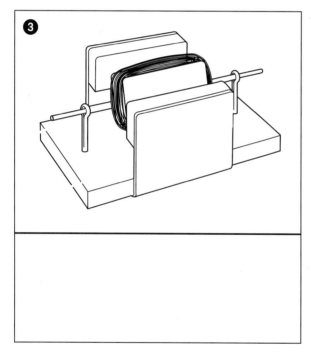

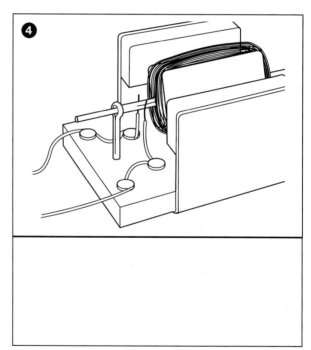

What happened?

When we switched on the power supply _____

_____

_____ .

22B Using magnets to make a motor

1 The diagrams on the other sheet show us how to make a motor.
Use these words to fill in the boxes.

Make two 'brushes' to touch the bare ends of the coil.

Push a thin rod through the coil. Put the coil between the two magnets.

Wind the plastic-coated wire around the frame to make a coil.

Put the two magnets in place.

2 On diagrams 1 , 3 and 4 shade the coil of wire in green.

3 On diagrams 2, 3 and 4 shade the magnets in pencil.

4 Complete the sentence at the bottom of the sheet in your own words.

23A Electricity for our homes

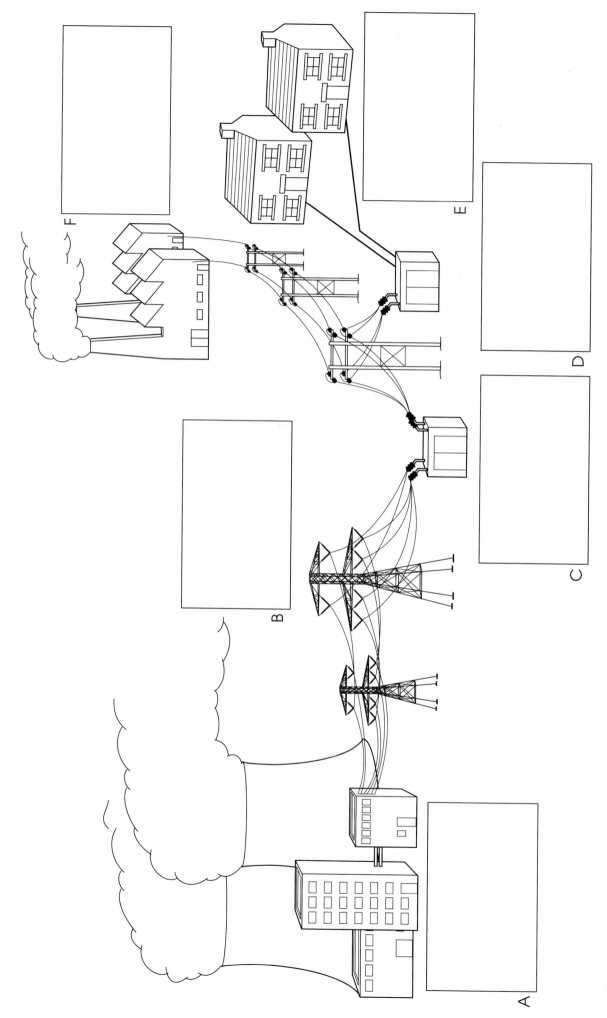

23B Electricity for our homes

1 Use these labels for the diagram on the other sheet.

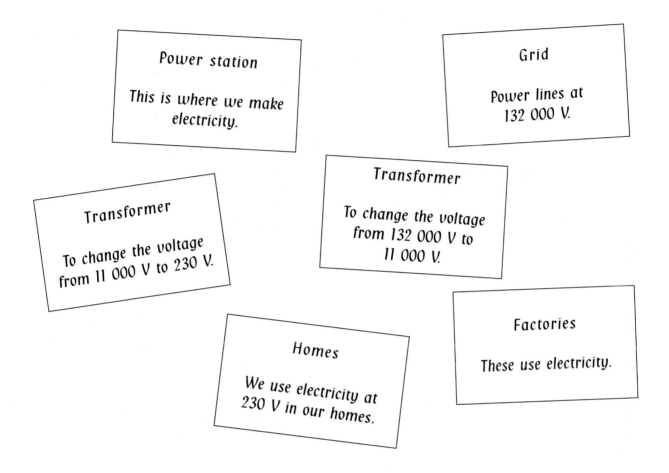

2 Shade the power station in red.

3 Shade the transformers in green.

4 Shade the homes in blue.

5 Shade the factories in pencil.

24 Using magnets to make electricity

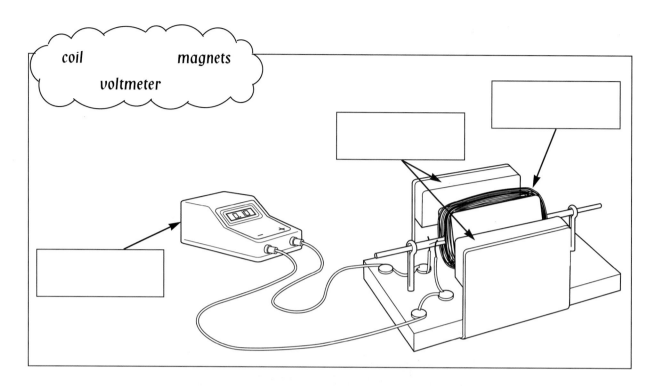

coil   magnets
    voltmeter

When we spin the coil between the magnets we make electricity.

1 We get a reading of _____ volts on the voltmeter.

2 If we want to make an even bigger voltage we need to:

- _____

- _____

- _____

3 We have made electricity using a dynamo.

Bicycles often have a dynamo to make _____

to light a _____ .

When the rider stops pedalling the _____ goes out.

This is because the _____ has stopped working.

Energy
and
the Earth

1 Energy word list

A air

B biomass

C cavity wall
chemical
coal
conduction
conductor
convection
curtains

D double glazing

E electrical
energy

F fibreglass

G gas
geothermal

H hydroelectric

I insulation
insulator

J

K

L lagging
light

M movement

N non-renewable
nuclear

O oil

P

Q

R radiation
rays
renewable
resources

S sound
stored

T temperature

U

V variable

W waste
wave
wind

X, Y, Z

2 Earth word list

A	**J** Jupiter	**Q**
B	**K**	**R** rocket
C	**L**	**S** satellite Saturn space Sun
D		
	M Mars Mercury moon	
E Earth		**T**
F	**N** Neptune	**U** Uranus
G gravity		**V** Venus
H	**O** orbit	**W**
	P planets Pluto	
I		**X, Y, Z**

3 Conduction

We can test how fast heat travels along a metal rod by using this apparatus.
When the heat from the flame reaches the pin, the wax melts and the pin
drops off.

copper rod

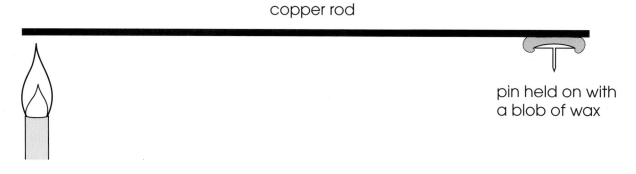

pin held on with
a blob of wax

❶ You want to find out which metal carries heat more quickly, aluminium or
copper. Which aluminium rod will you use?

Why did you choose it?

A _____ aluminium

B _____ aluminium

❷ What other things must you keep the same if you want to carry out
a fair test?

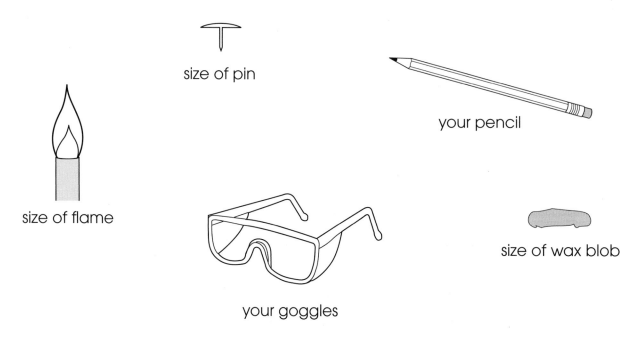

size of pin

your pencil

size of flame

your goggles

size of wax blob

4 Convection

• Put the right words under each diagram.

The cool water falls.	The warm water cools down at the top of the beaker.
The warm water rises.	The flame heats the water above it.

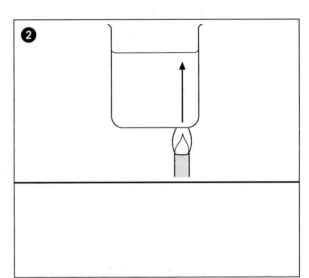

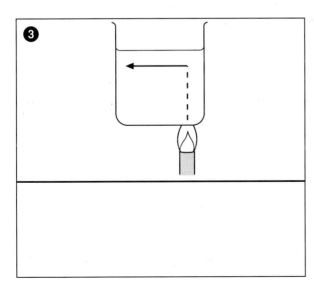

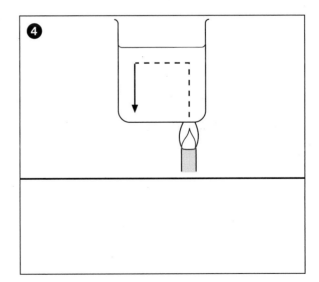

This is called a **convection** current.

5 Radiation

Heat can travel through empty space by heat rays or **infrared rays**.
We call this **radiation**.

We get heat from the Sun by radiation.

Infrared rays take eight minutes to get from the Sun to the Earth.

People often wear white clothes in summer. This is because white clothes reflect a lot of infrared rays. The best material to reflect the heat has a shiny surface. Fire-fighters often wear suits made out of shiny material.

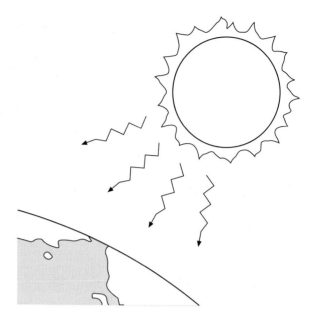

Radiation

Another name for heat rays is ...	
Heat rays can travel through ...	
Heat from the Sun travels to Earth by ...	
White clothes keep you cool in summer because ...	
The best surface to reflect infrared rays is ...	

6 Heat moving

- Match these words with the meanings below.

> conduction
>
> radiation
>
> convection

Meanings

A   Heat energy travelling by rays. The rays travel very quickly.

This is called _____ .

B   Heat energy travelling by being passed from one particle to the next.

This is called _____ .

C   Heat energy travelling by warming up the air or water around it.
Warm air or water rises.

This is called _____ .

The spoon handle getting warm.

_____

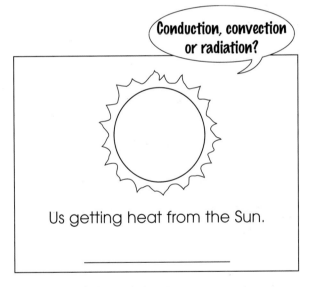

Conduction, convection or radiation?

Us getting heat from the Sun.

_____

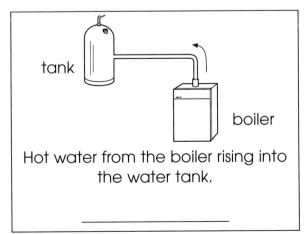

tank

boiler

Hot water from the boiler rising into
the water tank.

_____

Heating water in a pan.

_____

7 What changes?

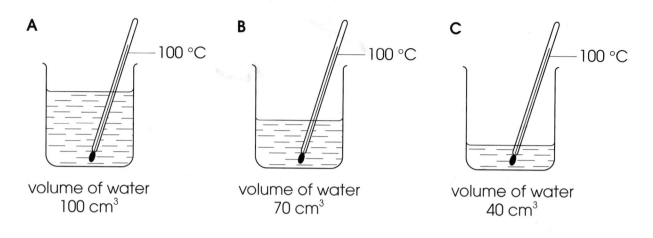

A
100 °C

volume of water
100 cm³

B
100 °C

volume of water
70 cm³

C
100 °C

volume of water
40 cm³

The beakers of water are different because _____

_____

_____ .

Look at the table.

Beaker	Temperature at start (°C)	Temperature after 10 mins (°C)
A	100	75
B	100	60
C	100	45

After 10 minutes the beakers of water are different because _____

_____

_____ .

The **volume** and the **temperature** of the water are the **factors** which
change or are different.

8A Insulating the home

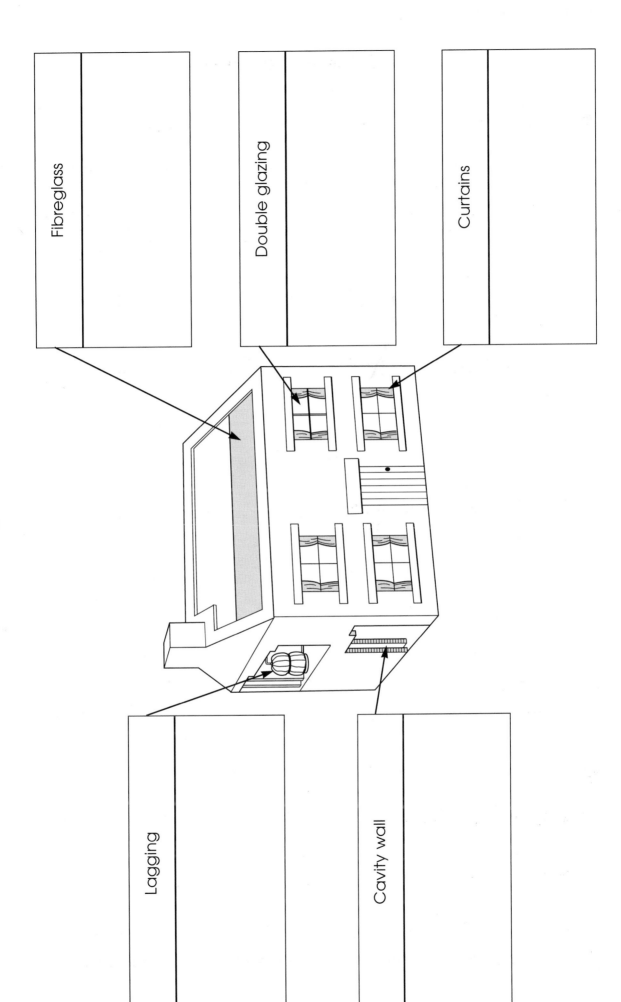

Fibreglass

Double glazing

Curtains

Lagging

Cavity wall

Science Support: Physics © Cambridge University Press, 1997

8B Insulating the home

1 Use these words to complete the diagram on the other sheet.

> This often contains foam. The foam traps air.

> This traps a layer of air between two pieces of glass.

> Closing these at night keeps more heat in the room.

> This traps air in the fibres. It stops heat from escaping through the roof.

> This stops heat escaping from the hot water tank.

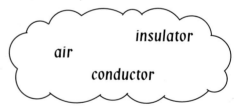

insulator

air

conductor

2 Complete these sentences.

Many kinds of insulation work by trapping _____ .

Air is a poor _____ of heat.

We say that it is a good _____ .

9 To lag or not to lag?

Both of these tanks are full of water. We heat the water up to 60 °C.

Then we turn off the heaters.

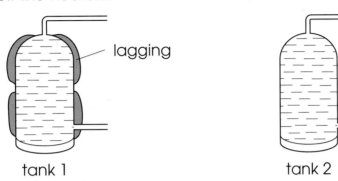

lagging

tank 1   tank 2

• The water will cool down most quickly in tank _____ .

The graph tells us the temperature in tank 1 for the next six hours.

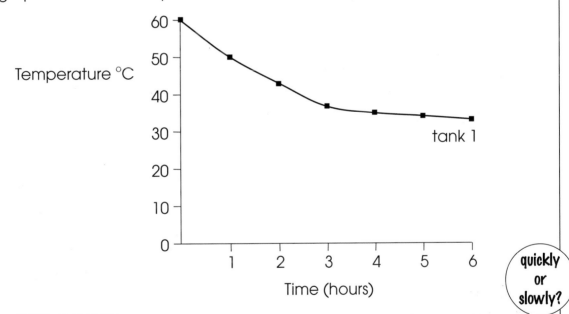

Temperature °C

Time (hours)

tank 1

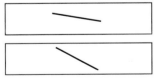 quickly or slowly?

A shallow line means cooling down _____ .

A steep line means cooling down _____ .

❶ After six hours the water in tank 2 will be (**warmer than / cooler than / the same as**) the water in tank 1.

❷ Remember both tanks started at the same temperature. Draw a line on the graph to show how the water in tank 2 might cool down.

10 Energy transfer

m	s	u	e	t	c	v	w
l	t	r	l	s	h	d	x
m	o	v	e	m	e	n	t
k	r	q	c	p	m	u	y
j	e	n	t	o	l	o	z
i	d	m	r	f	c	s	a
t	h	g	i	l	a	g	h
h	j	e	c	e	l	d	i
g	k	l	a	t	c	b	b
f	e	d	l	t	n	o	a

Types of energy

Electrical energy can be transferred into many useful kinds of energy.

Electricity transfers energy in the home.

 Electrical energy is transferred into _____ energy.

 Electrical energy is transferred into _____ energy.

 Electrical energy is transferred into _____ energy.

 Electrical energy is transferred into _____ energy.

11A Keeping the water warm

In your home, the water heater heats up the hot water in your tank. You need this water to stay warm all day. The tank is made from copper.

Find out which is the best material to cover the tank to keep the water warm. You can use these materials.

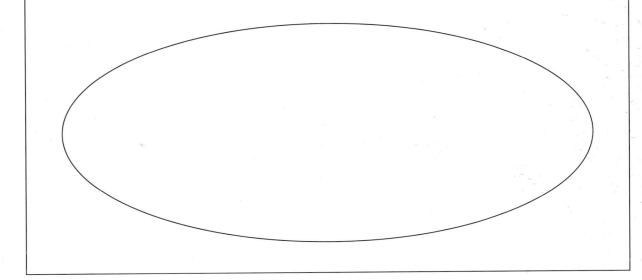

Aim

What are you trying to find out?

Method (What you are going to do)

1 How will you set up your apparatus?

2 How will you carry out the experiment?

3 What measurements will you take?

4 How will you make sure that you do a fair test?

5 What will you do to make sure that the experiment is safe?

6 Which material do you think will be best at keeping the water warm?

Results

How will you record your results?

11B Keeping the water warm

Read the bubble below.

> Two thin layers of material are better at keeping water warm than one thick layer.

Find out if this is **true** or **false**. The material you can use is

Aim

What are you trying to find out?

Method (What you are going to do)

How will you test this out?

Results

How will you record your results?

12 Wasting energy

A runner

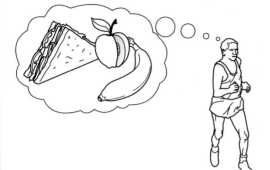

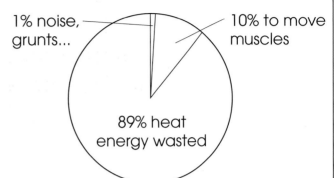

1% noise, grunts...

10% to move muscles

89% heat energy wasted

❶ The runner gets his energy from _____ .

❷ On the pie chart:

a shade in blue the energy the runner uses to move his body.

b shade in red the energy that his body wastes as heat.

A power station

35% useful electrical energy

65% heat energy wasted

❸ The power station gets its energy from _____ .

❹ On the pie chart:

a shade in blue the energy that is used to make electricity.

b shade in red the energy that is wasted at the power station.

When we 'use' energy, most of it is lost.

Most energy is wasted as _____ energy.

13 Keeping warm

We can use a graph to tell us how warm a room is at different times in the evening.

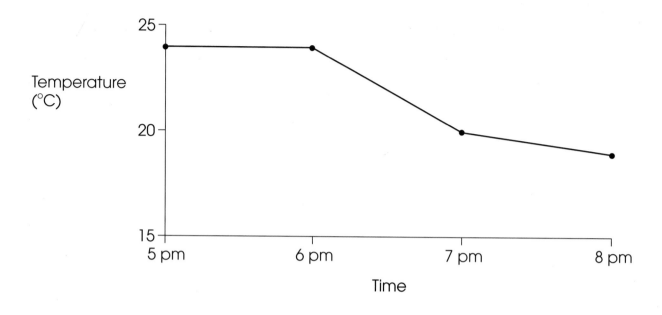

A shallow slope on the graph means the room is cooling down slowly.

A steep slope on the graph means _____

_____ .

• Use the graph to help you answer these questions.

❶ The heating was turned off in the room at _____ .

❷ Closing the curtains stopped the room from cooling down so fast. The

curtains were closed in the room at _____ .

14 Energy resources

- Copy the table. Fill it in using the words below.

Renewable energy	Non-renewable energy

We are running out of this.

This will not run out.

We get this from the Sun, the wind and the sea.

Coal, oil and gas give us this.

We get this from fuels which were made a long time ago.

It is often difficult to use this.

15 Renewable energy

h y d r o e l e c t r i c
a b c w d e f t b g h i r
s r q a p o n m i l k j a
t u v v d n i w o d w x e
h g f e d c b a m z a y l
g e o t h e r m a l t l c
i j k l m n o p s q r s u
z y x r a l o s s w v u n

Types of renewable energy

Type of renewable energy	How it works
	This uses the energy from the Sun.
	We get this energy when uranium atoms break up.
	When the tide goes in and out it gives us this energy.
	This uses the energy of waves.
	This uses the energy from the wind.
	This uses rotting plant and animal materials.
	This uses the heat from deep inside the Earth.
	This uses the energy from falling water.

16A Our planets

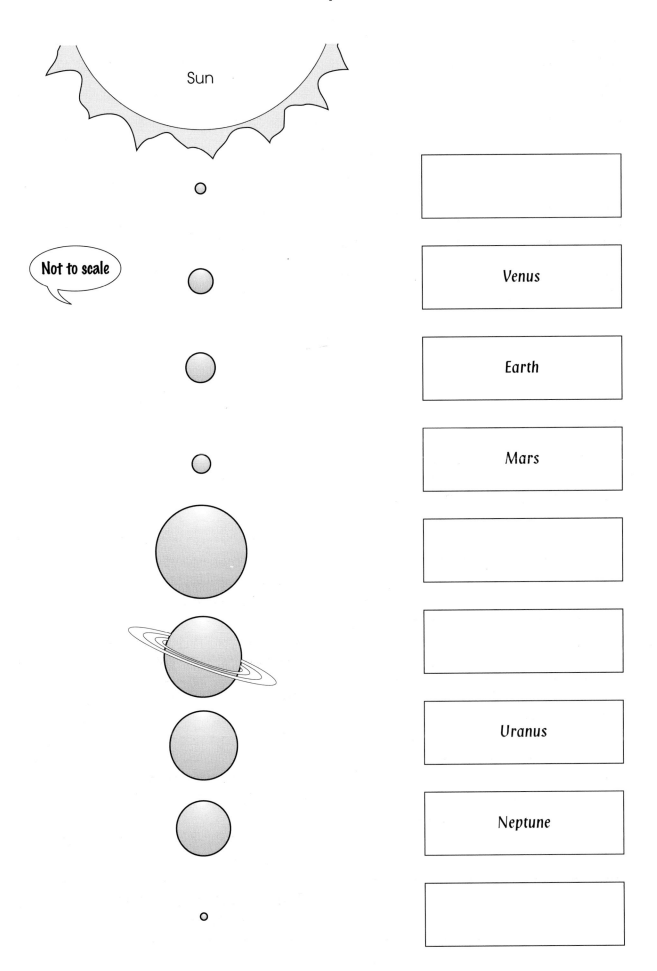

Sun

Not to scale

Venus

| Earth |

| Mars |

| Uranus |

| Neptune |

16B Our planets

Look at the other sheet.

1 Find the Sun. Shade it in yellow.

2 Mercury is the closest planet to the Sun. Shade it in red and label it.

3 Find the Earth. Shade it in green.

4 Jupiter is the biggest planet. Shade it in black and label it.

5 Saturn is a large planet with rings around it. Label it and go over the rings in yellow. Now shade it in pencil.

7 Pluto is the furthest planet from the Sun. Label it and shade it in blue.

7 Use your diagram to help you to complete this table.

Description of planet	Name of planet
We live on it.	
It is the closest planet to the Sun.	
It is the furthest planet from the Sun.	
It is the largest planet.	
It has rings around it.	

17 Planets wordsearch

Take care! The Sun is not a planet!

u	r	a	n	u	s	z	m
p	t	u	e	s	r	q	e
l	j	u	p	i	t	e	r
u	v	w	t	x	m	y	c
t	n	r	u	t	a	s	u
o	l	m	n	n	r	p	r
s	u	n	e	v	s	o	y
k	j	i	h	t	r	a	e

Planets

• Now put the planets in order, the one nearest to the Sun first and so on.

❶ _____

❷ _____   ❻ _____

❸ _____   ❼ _____

❹ _____   ❽ _____

❺ _____   ❾ _____

18A In orbit

Planets in orbit

There are nine planets that move around the Sun. We say that they **orbit** the Sun. One of these planets is Earth.

The Earth takes about 365 days to orbit the Sun. This is why there are 365 days in a year.

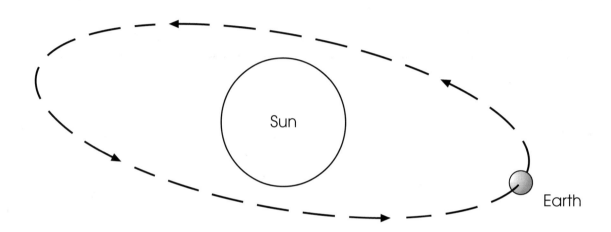

The moon in orbit

The Earth has one moon. The moon moves around the Earth.
It takes about 28 days (or a month) for the moon to orbit the Earth.

Some of the other planets have also got moons that orbit them.
Saturn has 18 moons!

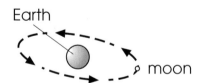

18B In orbit – linkword

1. Cut out each of the word patches below.

2. Arrange them on a large piece of paper.

3. Draw lines between the words if you can think of something that links them.

4. Write on the lines if it makes the link clearer.

Example:

has one

| Earth | ⟶ | moon |

5. When you have made as many links as you can, stick the word patches down on the paper.

---

orbits
(moves around)

month

Sun

moon

Earth

planets

year

19A Satellites

Hundreds of satellites have been put into space. They have been put there by rockets. Some of them move around the Earth.

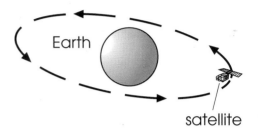

We say that these satellites **orbit** the Earth.

If a satellite is a long way from the Earth, it takes a long time to orbit.

A closer satellite orbits the Earth more quickly.

Satellites are very useful

Satellites can pass telephone messages from one side of the Earth to another. The Telecom satellite does this.

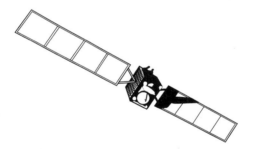

Satellites like SPOT can take photographs of the Earth's surface.

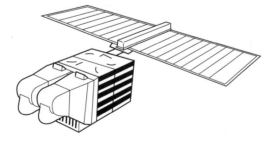

Satellites can tell us about the weather on the Earth. Meteosat is a weather satellite.

19B Satellites

- Use the other sheet to help you complete the table below.

To put satellites into space we use...	
We say that satellites orbit the Earth. This means that...	
The closer a satellite is to the Earth the...	
We use the Telecom satellite to...	
We use the SPOT satellite to...	
We use the Meteosat satellite to...	

Science Support: Physics © Cambridge University Press, 1997

Forces and motion

1 Forces and motion word list

A acceleration
accelerating

B brake

C

D decelerating
distance

E elastic
electrostatic

F fast
forces
friction

G gravity

H hydraulic

I

J

K

L liquid

M magnetic
mass
metre
movement

N Newton
Newtometer

O

P pressure
push
pull

Q

R resistance

S second
speed
stopping
syringe

T ticker timer
trolley

U

V

W

X, Y, Z

2 Which force?

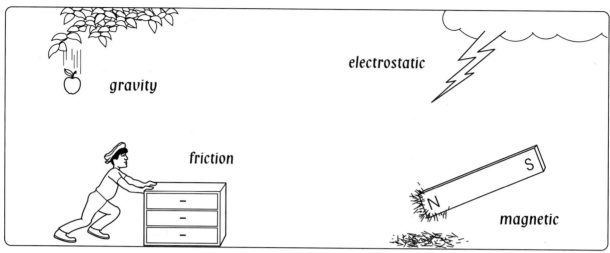

This force makes a balloon stick on the ceiling.

_____

This force pulls things towards the Earth.

_____

This force slows down moving objects.

_____

This force gives you weight.

_____

This force makes things wear out.

_____

This force makes your hair stand up.

_____

This force can be used to pick up scrap iron.

_____

This force is a pull, but only when you use a North
and a South pole.

_____

This force is greater on the Earth than on the moon.

_____

This force can be reduced by oiling the surfaces.

_____

This force makes a compass work.

_____

3A Forces and movement

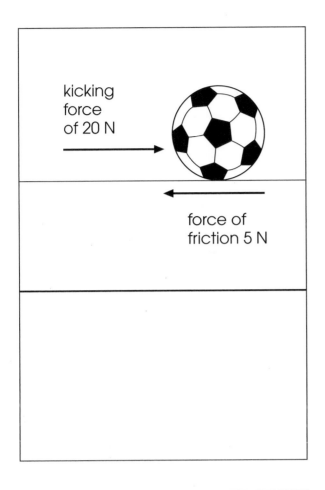

kicking force of 20 N

force of friction 5 N

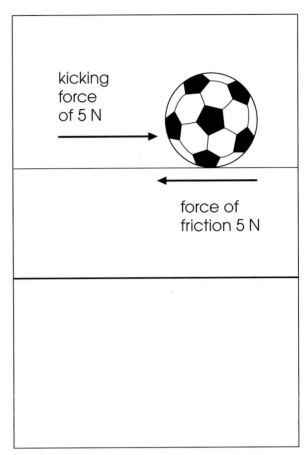

kicking force of 5 N

force of friction 5 N

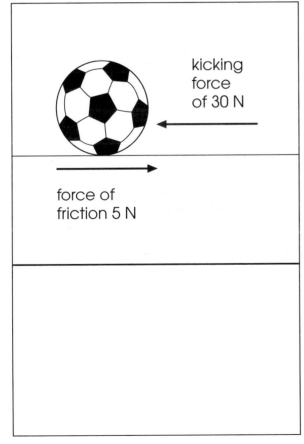

kicking force of 30 N

force of friction 5 N

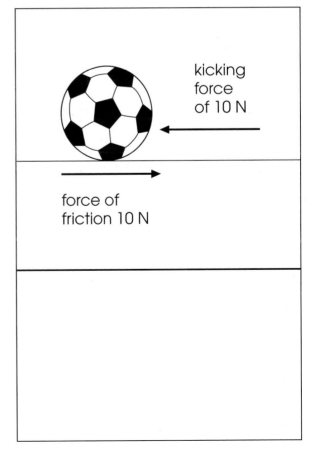

kicking force of 10 N

force of friction 10 N

3B Forces and movement

1 Choose the correct words to put under each diagram on the other sheet. Then complete the sentence.

The ball does not move because ...

The ball moves in this direction because ...

The ball moves in this direction because ...

The ball does not move because ...

2 On the other sheet, draw over the arrows that show the kicking force in red.

3 Using blue, draw over the arrows that show the force of friction.

4 Put a green box around those diagrams where the ball does not move at all.

5 Complete these sentences:

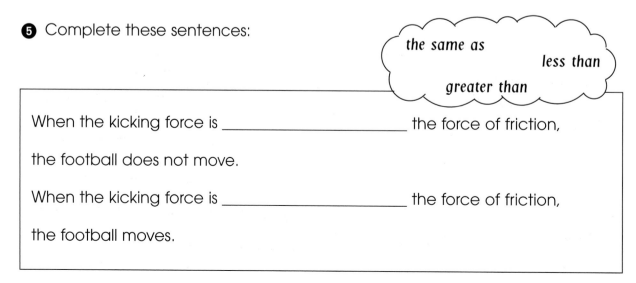

the same as

less than

greater than

When the kicking force is _____ the force of friction,

the football does not move.

When the kicking force is _____ the force of friction,

the football moves.

4 Friction

• Copy the table. Fill it in using the words below.

Useful things about friction	Where friction is a nuisance

Friction wears things out.

Friction with the air can make cars slow down.

Friction with the air means that a parachute drops slowly.

Friction stops you from slipping over.

Friction in the brakes makes a bike slow down.

If we rub our hands together they get hot. This helps to warm us up.

Friction helps tyres to grip the road.

Friction can make machines get too hot.

5 How fast?

> *speed*   *distance*   *time*
>
>   *tape measure*
>
>   *stopwatch*

We can find out how fast a person is running. We call this their _____ .

First we measure **how far** the person has run, or the _____ .

To do this we use a _____ .

Next we find out **how long** the person took, or the _____ .

To do this we use a _____ .

To work out a person's speed we do this calculation:

     speed = distance ÷ time

Example: If Kerry runs 80 metres in 10 seconds, what is her speed?

     speed = distance ÷ time

          =   80   ÷   10

        = 8 metres per second

        <u>or 8 m/s</u>

- What is the speed of these runners?

a   Sam runs 250 m in 50 seconds.

b   Julie runs 400 m in 80 seconds.

c   Karl runs 100 m in 10 seconds.

6 Graphs of moving things

Louise sets off from home and runs down the garden path.

After 10 seconds she stops to stroke the cat.

She strokes the cat for 20 seconds and then carries on walking down the path.

We can see this information in the graph below.

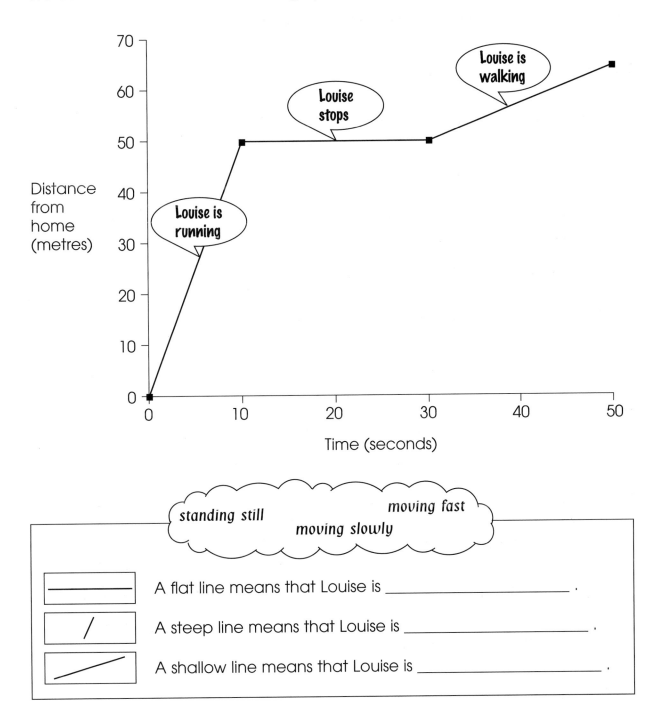

A flat line means that Louise is _____ .

A steep line means that Louise is _____ .

A shallow line means that Louise is _____ .

7 More graphs of moving things

A bus sets off from the bus station. The table tells us how it travels
for the next 30 minutes.

Time (minutes)	Distance from bus station (km)
0	0
10	3
15	3
30	4

1 Put the information from the table onto the graph below.

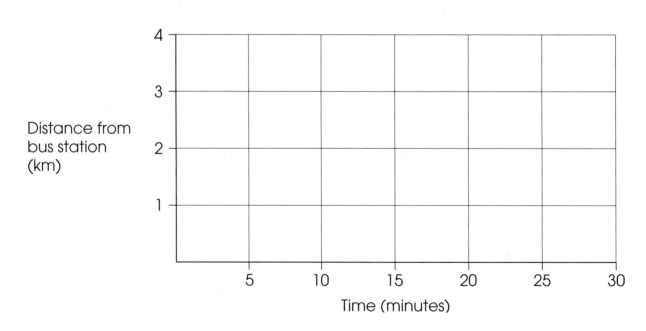

Distance from bus station (km)

Time (minutes)

2 On the graph, label when the bus:

a stopped moving,

b was travelling fast,

c was travelling slowly.

8A Using a ticker timer

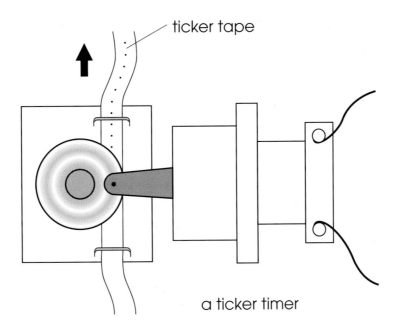

ticker tape

a ticker timer

❶ Pull the tape through the timer at a steady speed. Try not to speed up or slow down.

❷ Stick some of the tape in here.

❸ The dots are

_____ .

evenly spaced
getting further apart
getting closer together

❹ Pull the tape faster and faster (make it accelerate).

❺ Stick some of the tape in here.

❻ The dots start off

_____

closer together
further apart
evenly spaced

and then they get _____ .

8B Using a ticker timer

A

B

C

This shows something moving at a steady speed
(not speeding up or slowing down).

This shows something getting faster (**accelerating/decelerating**).

This shows something slowing down (**accelerating/decelerating**).

9A Getting faster

Making a trolley accelerate

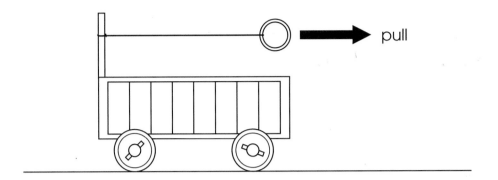

1 Set up a ticker timer.

2 Join some ticker tape to the trolley.

3 Pull the trolley with a steady force.
(Try to keep the **stretch** on the elastic the same.)

4 Make a ticker tape chart like this. Each piece of tape has
the same number of dots .

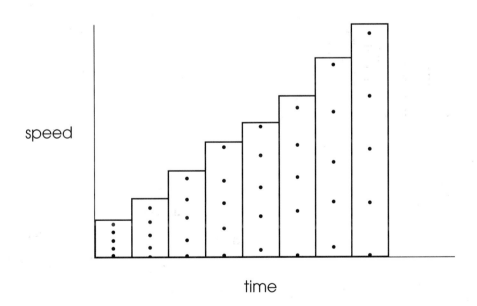

Your chart should go up in equal steps if you kept pulling with the same force.

The force on the trolley made it get faster (**accelerate**).

9B Getting faster

What happens if we use more force?

1 Now make a chart to show what happens if you pull with two pieces of elastic. This pulls the trolley with a bigger force.

2 Repeat with three pieces of elastic.

3 Your three charts should look like the ones below.

Use these words to label the charts.

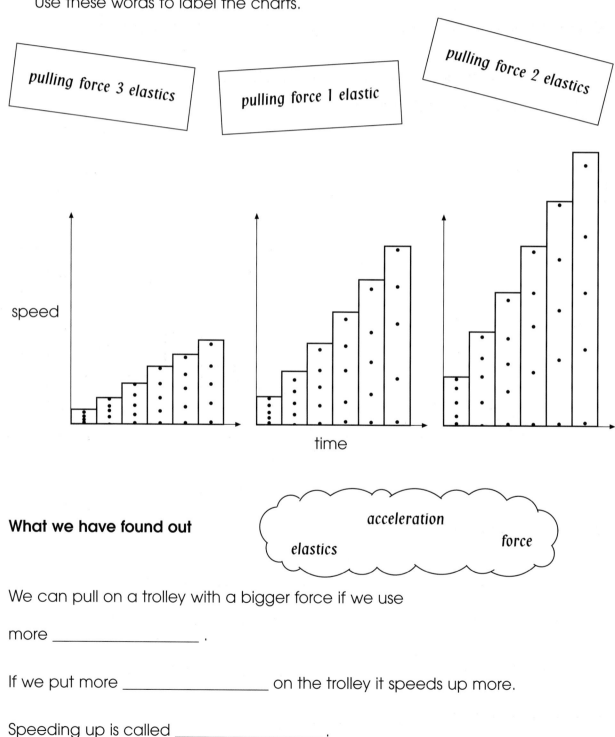

What we have found out

acceleration

elastics

force

We can pull on a trolley with a bigger force if we use

more _____ .

If we put more _____ on the trolley it speeds up more.

Speeding up is called _____ .

9C Getting faster

What happens if we give the trolley more mass?

We can give the trolley more mass like this.

❶ Now make a chart to show what happens if you pull a trolley that has twice the mass.

❷ Repeat with a trolley with three times the mass (put another on top!).

❸ Your three charts should look like the ones below.

Use these words to label the charts.

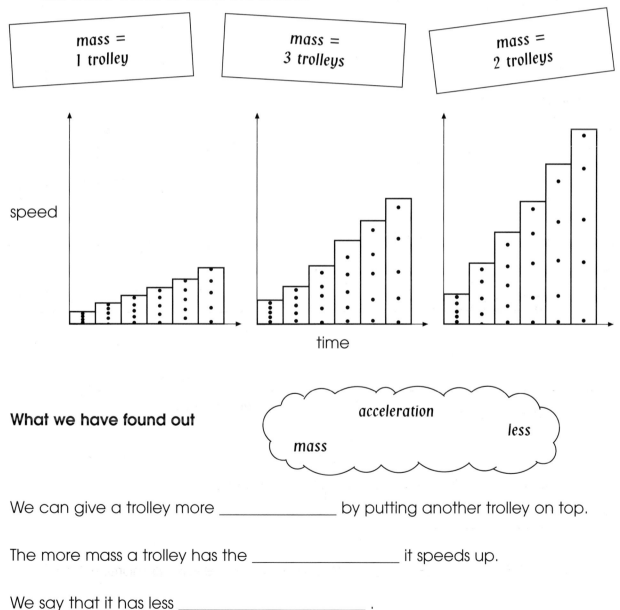

What we have found out

acceleration

less

mass

We can give a trolley more _____ by putting another trolley on top.

The more mass a trolley has the _____ it speeds up.

We say that it has less _____ .

10A Stopping distance

Imagine you are driving a car. When you put the brakes on, the car doesn't stop straight away. It takes some time to stop. The distance you travel before you stop is called the **stopping distance**.

Lots of things can affect the stopping distance.

❶ How hard you brake

If you put the brakes on with a big force, you stop quickly.
You have a short stopping distance.

If you only use a small force, the car will travel a long way before it stops.
You have a long stopping distance.

❷ How heavy the car is

A car full of passengers is heavy. It will not stop as quickly as when it is empty.
A heavy vehicle has a long stopping distance.

❸ The speed that you are travelling

If you are going fast and you put on the brakes, you will travel a long way before you stop.

Speed that you are travelling (km/h)	Stopping distance (m)
20	7
40	16
60	34
80	53
100	77
120	107

This is the length of a football pitch.

10B Stopping distance

Use the other sheet to help you answer these questions.

1 Underline in black the sentence that tells you what the stopping distance is.

2 Put a box around three things that can affect your stopping distance.

3 Underline in red what happens to your stopping distance if you brake with a small force.

4 Underline in blue what happens to your stopping distance if your vehicle is heavy.

5 Finish off the chart below using the information from the table.

The chart shows how the _____ of a car affects its

_____ _____ .

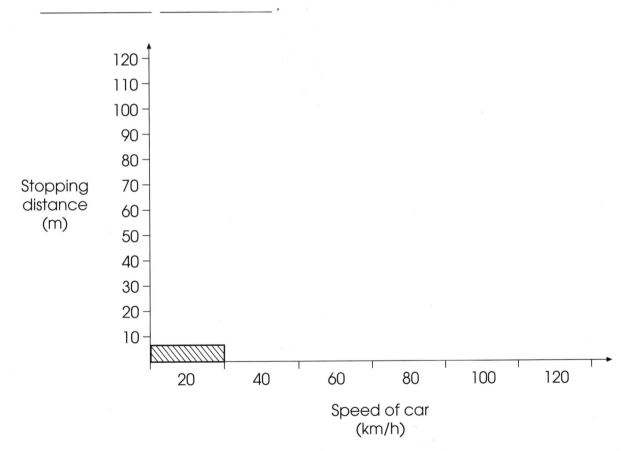

6 Complete this sentence.

The faster the car is travelling, the _____ the stopping distance.

11A Falling objects

When things fall, gravity makes them get faster and faster.

• We say that they **accelerate**.

11B Falling objects

❶ Label the diagram on the other sheet using these words.

| speed of coconut 5 m/s | speed of coconut 10 m/s | speed of coconut 20 m/s |

| speed of feather 1 m/s | speed of feather 2 m/s | speed of feather 3 m/s |

❷

gravity   resistance

less

slowly

faster

air

The coconut got _____ and _____ as it fell.

The speed of the feather was _____ than the speed of the

coconut. It fell more _____ . This was because the feather

was slowed down by the _____ of the _____ .

The force which made the feather and the coconut fall

is called _____ .

12 Gravity – linkword

❶ Cut out each of the word patches below.

❷ Arrange them on a large piece of paper.

❸ Draw lines between the words if you can think of something that links them.

❹ Write on the lines if it makes the link clearer.

Example:

is a type of

| gravity | → | force |

❺ When you have made as many links as you can, stick the word patches down on the paper.

mass

newtons

kilograms

gravity

moon

force

Earth

pull

weight

13A Pressure in liquids

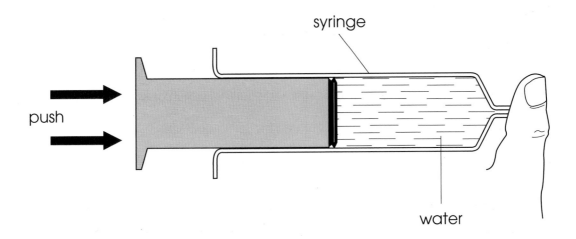

syringe

push

water

We cannot squash the water in the syringe, even if we push quite hard.

We cannot squeeze liquids like water into a smaller space. This can be very useful to us. We can use liquids to change a small force into a large force.

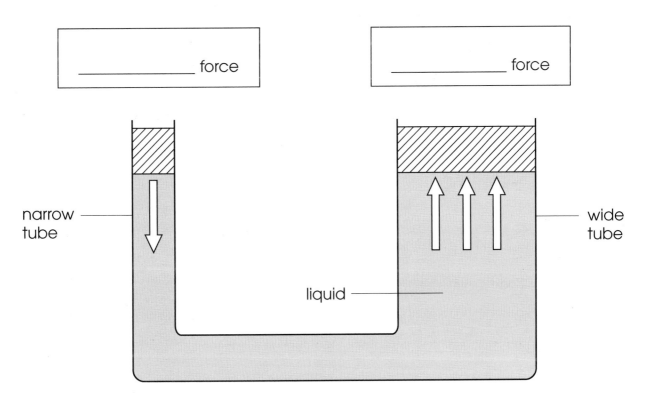

_____ force

_____ force

narrow tube

wide tube

liquid

In the narrow tube, the small force makes a high pressure in the liquid.

The high pressure moves through the liquid into the wide tube.
It makes a large force.

We call this a **hydraulic system**.

Hydraulic systems are used in car brakes and for lifting heavy loads.

13B Pressure in liquids

Look at the other sheet.

1 Find the water in the syringe. Shade it in blue.

2 Find the words which tell us what happens when we push on the syringe. Underline them in black.

Look at the second diagram.

3 Shade the liquid in yellow.

4 Label the forces with these words.

5 The arrows show the direction of the forces. Shade them in green.

6 Find the words which tell you what happens in the narrow tube. Underline them in red.

7 Find the words which tell you what happens in the wide tube. Underline them in blue.

8 Put a circle around the name that we give to this system.

9 Put a star (✱) above the things that use hydraulic systems.

Waves
and
radiation

1 Waves and radiation word list

A alpha
amplitude
angle
anvil

B beta
bend
blue

C cochlea
crest

D detect

E electromagnetic
energy

F

G gamma
green

H hammer

I indigo
infrared

J

K

L light

M microwaves
mirror

N normal

O orange

P pinna
prism

Q

R radio
radioactivity
radiation
ray
reflect
reflection

S sound
spectrum
stirrup
straight

T trough

U ultrasound
ultraviolet

V violet
visible

W wave
wavelength

X X-ray

Y yellow

Z

2A Mirrors

This diagram shows you how a mirror reflects a ray of light.

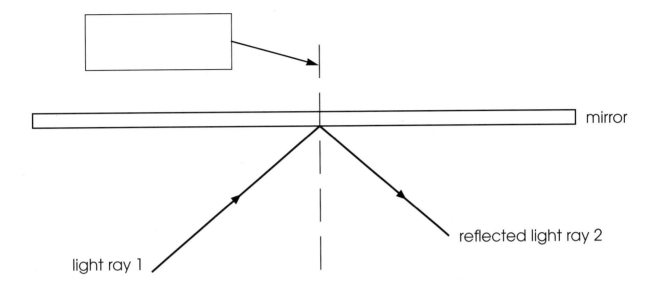

The angle between light ray 1 and the normal is _____ degrees.

The angle between light ray 2 and the normal is _____ degrees.

I notice that the two angles are _____ .

2B Mirrors

Look at the diagram on the other sheet.

❶ Carefully shade the mirror in pencil.

❷ Find the light ray that is travelling towards the mirror. Draw over it in red.

❸ Draw over the reflected light ray in blue.

❹ The dashed line is the **normal**. Draw over it in black. Label it.

❺ Measure the angle between the normal and light ray 1.

❻ Measure the angle between the normal and light ray 2.

❼ Fill in the gaps in the box below the diagram.

3A Light rays bending

This diagram shows you what happens when a ray of light travels from air into glass.

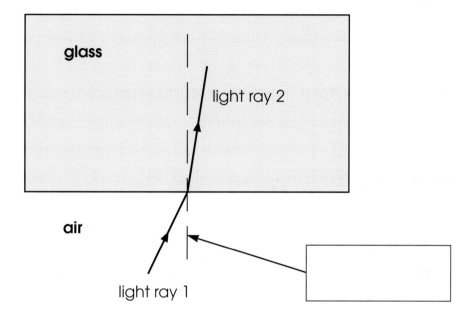

Light ray 1 is travelling in _____ .

The angle between light ray 1 and the normal is _____ degrees.

Light ray 2 is travelling in _____ .

The angle between light ray 2 and the normal is _____ degrees.

3B Light rays bending

Look at the diagram on the other sheet.

❶ Draw around the glass block in green.

❷ Find the light ray that is travelling in air. Draw over it in red.

❸ Find the light ray that is travelling in glass. Draw over it in blue.

❹ The dashed line is the **normal**. Draw over it in black. Label it.

❺ Measure the angle between the normal and light ray 1.

❻ Measure the angle between the normal and light ray 2.

❼ Fill in the gaps in the box below the diagram.

❽ Complete these sentences:

When light rays travel from air into glass they bend.
They bend (**towards/away from**) the normal.

4A Splitting up white light

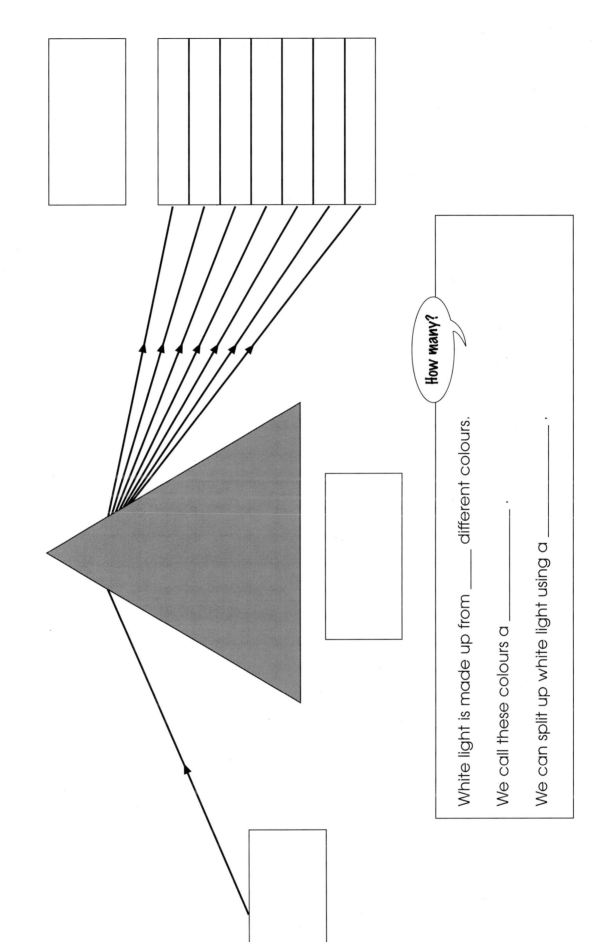

How many?

White light is made up from ＿＿＿ different colours.

We call these colours a ＿＿＿＿＿＿.

We can split up white light using a ＿＿＿＿＿＿.

4B Splitting up white light

1 Complete the diagram on the other sheet using these labels.

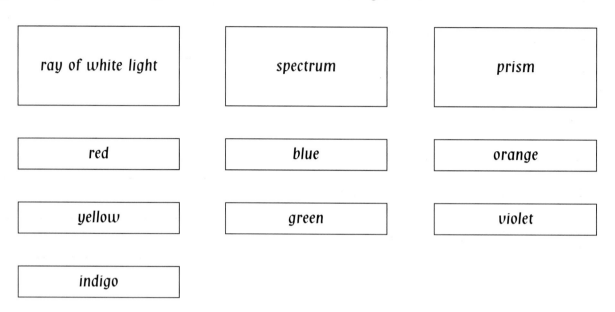

ray of white light	spectrum	prism
red	blue	orange
yellow	green	violet
indigo		

2 Draw around the prism in black.

Indigo is dark blue.

3 Using the right colours, shade in the spectrum.

4 Now look at the box below the diagram. Fill in the gaps in the sentences.

5 Lightword

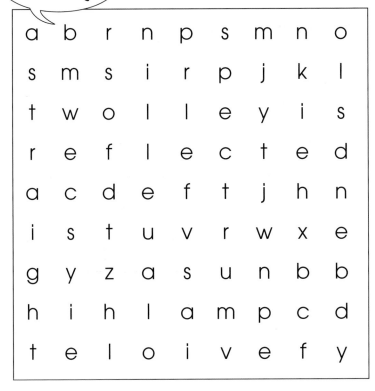

Find nine words to do with light.

a	b	r	n	p	s	m	n	o
s	m	s	i	r	p	j	k	l
t	w	o	l	l	e	y	i	s
r	e	f	l	e	c	t	e	d
a	c	d	e	f	t	j	h	n
i	s	t	u	v	r	w	x	e
g	y	z	a	s	u	n	b	b
h	i	h	l	a	m	p	c	d
t	e	l	o	i	v	e	f	y

• Now match the words with the sentences below.

❶ When a light ray hits a mirror it is _____ .

❷ When a light ray moves from air into glass it _____ .

❸ To split up white light we use a _____ .

❹ White light is made from red, orange, _____ , green, blue,

indigo and _____ .

❺ We call these seven colours a _____ .

❻ Light travels in _____ lines.

❼ Two sources of light are the _____ and a _____ .

6 Sound and light

• Copy the table. Fill it in using the words below.

Sound waves	Light waves

They travel 330 metres in one second.

They are detected by the eye.

They travel 300 000 000 metres in one second.

These come from the Sun and a candle.

These travel in straight lines.

These carry sound energy.

They are detected by the ear.

These can bend around corners.

These carry light energy.

7A Waves

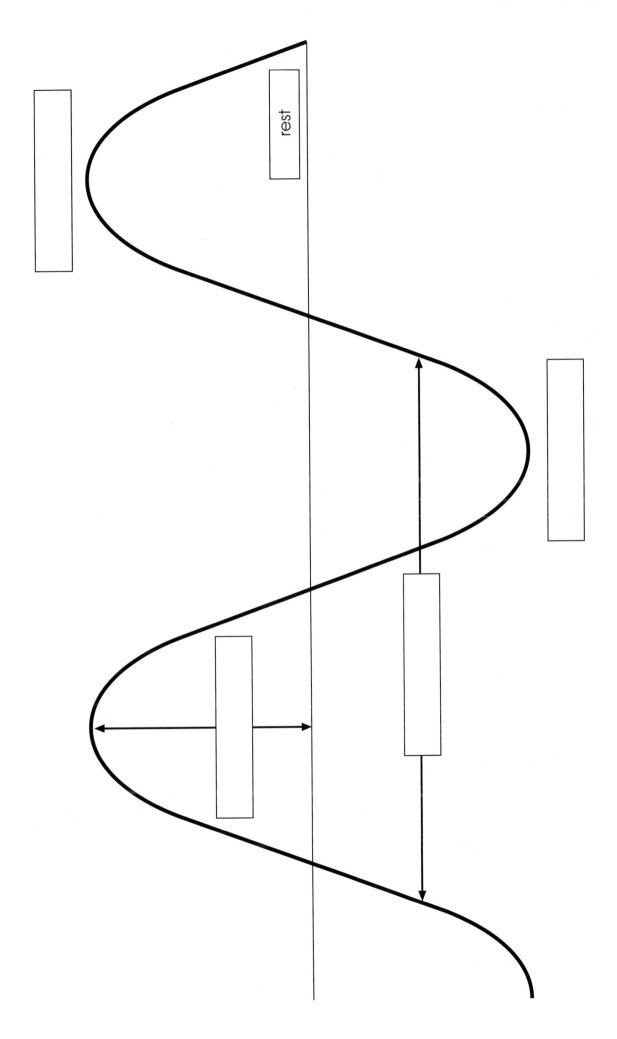

rest

7B Waves

Look at the diagram on the other sheet.

❶ Trace over the wave in red.

❷ A **crest** is the highest point a wave reaches. Label a crest.

❸ A **trough** is the lowest point a wave reaches. Label a trough.

❹ The **amplitude** is the distance from rest to a crest (or rest to a trough). Label the amplitude.

❺ The **wavelength** is the distance from one point on a wave to the same point on the next wave. Label the wavelength.

Part of wave	What it is
amplitude	
crest	
trough	
wavelength	

8A The ear

Too much noise can damage these parts of the ear.

Key

Science Support: Physics © Cambridge University Press, 1997

8B The ear

❶ Label the diagram on the other sheet using these words.

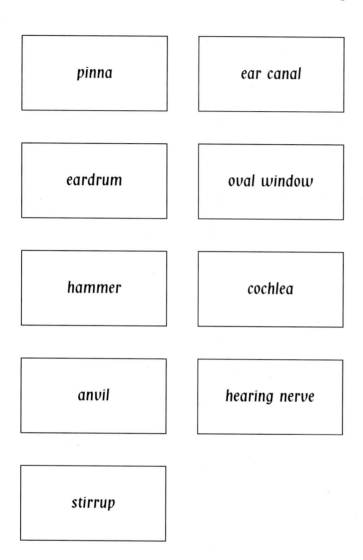

pinna	ear canal
eardrum	oval window
hammer	cochlea
anvil	hearing nerve
stirrup	

❷ Too much noise can damage the **eardrum** and the **cochlea**.

Show this on the diagram by shading in the labels and the key to match.

9A Ultrasound

There are some sound waves that we can't hear. We call them **ultrasound** waves. Ultrasound is very useful to us.

An ultrasound scanner can tell us about a baby before it is born.
The scanner sends ultrasound waves into the mother's body.
We can see a picture of the baby and find out if it is growing well.

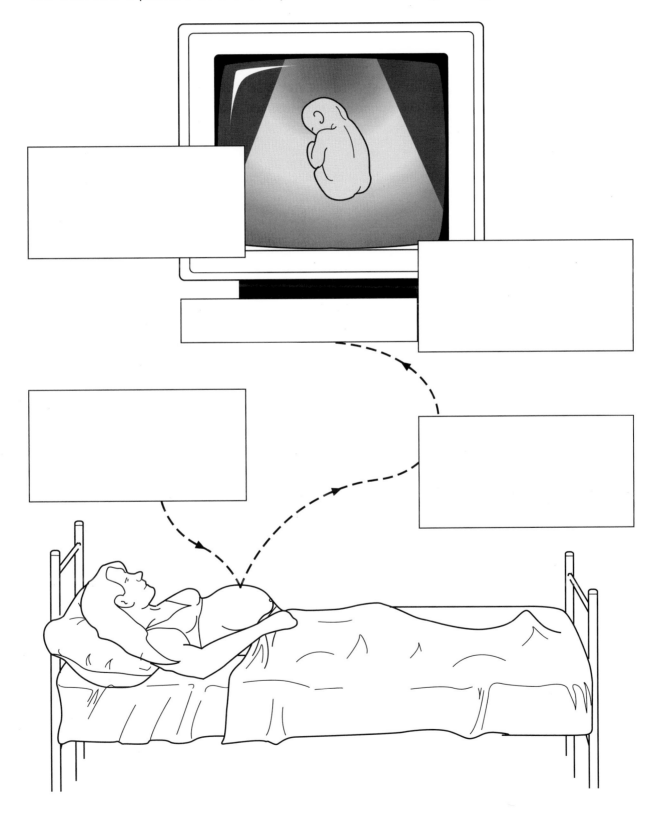

9B Ultrasound

Look at the other sheet.

❶ Underline in red the name of the sound waves that we can't hear.

❷ Underline in blue what an ultrasound scanner can do.

❸ Use these labels to complete the diagram.

We send ultrasound waves into the mother's body.	Some of the ultrasound waves are bounced back (reflected)
We see a picture of the unborn baby on the screen.	The computer makes sense of the reflected ultrasound waves.

❹ Find the line that shows the ultrasound waves passing into the mother's body. Draw over it in green.

❺ Find the line that shows the reflected ultrasound waves. Draw over it in red.

❻ Label the computer.

10 Electromagnetic waves

- Match the waves with the boxes which describe them.

long wavelength		short wavelength

radio waves

infrared rays

visible light rays

ultraviolet rays

X-rays

gamma rays

Given out by warm objects.
We can detect these rays using our skin or a thermometer.

Given out by the Sun.
These dangerous rays can damage our skin (sunburn).

Given out by lamps and the Sun.
We can detect these rays with the film in a camera and with our eyes.

Given out by a transmitter.
To pick up these waves we need an aerial and a receiver.

Given out by radioactive substances.
These rays are dangerous. We can only detect them using a Geiger-Müller tube.

Given out by an X-ray tube.
These rays are dangerous. They can be picked up using the film in a camera.

11 Useful waves

There are many types of waves. Some of them belong to a group called the **electromagnetic spectrum**. They can be very useful to us.

• Match the waves below with their uses.

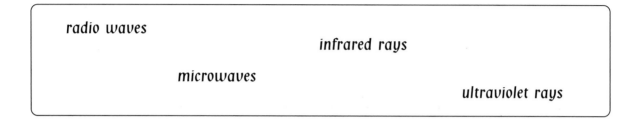

radio waves

infrared rays

microwaves

ultraviolet rays

These waves can travel hundreds of kilometres. They carry radio and television messages.

We use these waves to heat things up, e.g. for making toast. They are the same as heat rays.

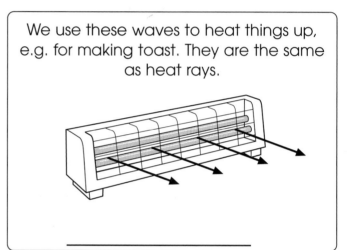

We can get a sun-tan from these waves. They come from the Sun.

These waves can cook food. They are made by a special kind of cooker. If these waves escape from the cooker they can be dangerous.

12 Waveword

Clues across

1 We can split visible light into red, orange, yellow, _____ , blue, indigo and violet light. (5)

3 These rays can be dangerous. They can cause skin cancer. (11)

4 These rays are used to photograph our bones. (5)

5 Radio waves have a _____ wavelength. (4)

6 Gamma waves have a _____ wavelength. (5)

7 These waves are used to heat up our food quickly. (10)

Clue down

2 Radio, infrared, visible light, ultraviolet, X-rays and gamma rays all belong to the _____ spectrum. (15)

13A Types of radioactivity

Alpha particles

These particles are made up from two protons and two neutrons.
Alpha particles travel at high speed. They can be stopped by a thin sheet of paper or by your skin.

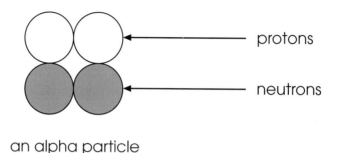

protons

neutrons

an alpha particle

Beta particles

Beta particles are fast-moving electrons. They travel at high speed. We can stop them using a thin sheet of metal.

a beta particle

Gamma rays

Gamma rays are waves. They are very dangerous. They travel at very high speed. They travel at the speed of light. We can only slow them down with very thick sheets of concrete.

a gamma ray

13B Types of radioactivity

- Use the other sheet to complete the table below.

Type of radioactivity	What it is made from	Speed that the radioactivity travels	How we can stop the radioactivity
alpha			
beta			
gamma			

- Now put a large red star by the most dangerous type of radioactivity.

Science Support: Physics © Cambridge University Press, 1997

14 Using radioactivity

• Copy the table. Fill it in using the words below.

Useful things about radioactivity	Why radioactivity can be harmful

Radiation can harm human skin and tissue.

Doctors can use radioactivity to kill cancer cells.

Gamma rays can cause cancer.

We can check for leaks in pipes using radioactivity.

We can't see radioactivity if it leaks out.

We can use gamma rays to kill microbes in food.